Jesus Heals

Scripture text from
The Contemporary English Version

Master
Books

CHAPTER 1

Jesus
Heals

Peter Bruegel the Elder
(c. 1525-1569)
The Beggars
Painted on wood

What do you think the artist wants to say about the beggars? How does this picture make you feel about them?

© Photo RMN - Jean, Louvre, Paris (France)

What Jesus Did

A young Sri Lankan woman bathing

In his time Jesus encountered several people who struggled with life. Some people were lame, blind, deaf, and dumb, the others suffered from paralysis and leprosy. They had no choice except to beg for help. They were scared of doctors because, at that time, doctors sometimes had a bad reputation. People usually tried treatments with massages, ointments, washing in water, or going to healers who would lay hands on them to relieve their pain.

In the time of Jesus, many people believed that sickness or pain had its origin in an evil spirit which had taken over a person's body. So a complete healing included both taking away the disease and casting out this bad spirit, sometimes called a demon.

Jesus had pity on all the sick people he met. He wanted to take care of them. Some of them were cured and thanked God. Jesus was different from other healers of his day. He didn't use magic or ask people for money. He acted out of loving kindness when he healed.

Mark's Good News*

After the death and resurrection of Jesus, the people he had healed remembered what had happened to them. In the villages many people had stories about what Jesus did to help them or their relative. People were also beginning to discover more fully who Jesus really was. After more than forty years Mark wrote his Gospel. He called it: *The good news of Jesus Christ, the Son of God* (Mark 1.1). According to Mark, Jesus began his work in Galilee by calling disciples and by healing many people. Mark wants to show that Jesus' power to overcome the pain of sickness is part of the Good News.**

* Mark
Most schlars believe that Mark wrote the first Gospel, and that he did so between A.D. *60 and 70. He was not one of the disciples. He probably found out all about Jesus from Peter.*

** Other healings
In the first few pages of his Gospel, Mark tells us about other healings: a man who had been possessed by an evil spirit; a leper; a paralyzed man brought to Jesus by his four friends; a man with a crippled hand (Mark 1.14 – 3.12).

The open hands of a beggar

At Sunset

Mark 1.29-34

As soon as Jesus left the meeting place with James and John, they went home with Simon and Andrew. When they got there, Jesus was told that Simon's mother-in-law was sick in bed with fever. Jesus went to her. He took hold of her hand and helped her up. The fever left her, and she served them a meal.

That evening after sunset, all who were sick or had demons in them were brought to Jesus. In fact, the whole town gathered around the door of the house. Jesus healed all kinds of terrible diseases and forced out a lot of demons. But the demons knew who he was, and he did not let them speak.

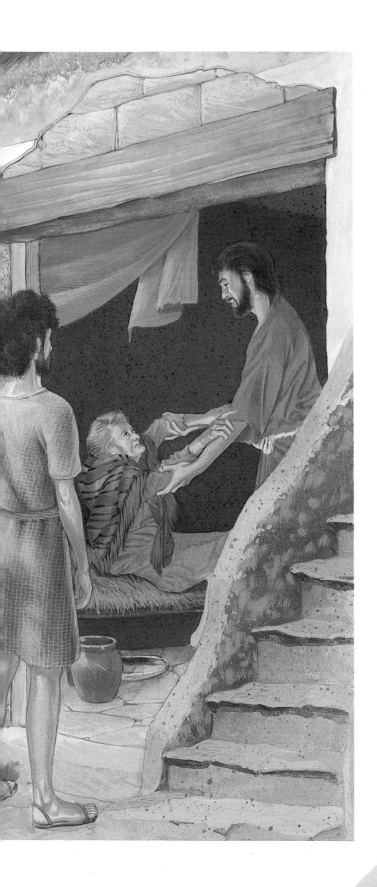

Meeting place

A synagogue (meeting place) where Jews went to pray and worship God. Mark is talking about the meeting place in the town of Capernaum, on the edge of Lake Tiberias. You can still visit the site and remains of this building today.

Home

Simon, who was also called Peter, lived near the meeting place. Jesus probably stayed at his house when he started his work in Capernaum.

Demons

In Mark's Gospel, demons are thought to be responsible for certain illnesses. They also represent the forces of evil that are opposed to Jesus.

The Struggle against Evil

Healing

Jesus was always full of compassion when he met sick and disabled people. Just being with him made them feel better. He always went out of his way to meet them so he could lessen their suffering and heal them. This is how he showed them that God cares about them and will not abandon them to the power of suffering.

Fighting Suffering

By taking care of those who suffer, Jesus took up the fight against suffering and everything that ruins peoples' lives and makes them unhappy. Jesus wanted to show that no one deserves to suffer, and that God stands alongside everyone who suffers!

Demons

The Bible describes several encounters that Jesus had with people who were demon-possessed. These demons — angels who had earlier rebelled with Satan against God — controlled humans and made them do wicked things. In casting out these demons from people, Jesus showed that he has complete power over every evil thing.

Back on Your Feet

When Jesus healed people he had one purpose in mind: to get them back on their feet! He was trying to free them from the pain and suffering that pulled them down and cut them off from life and others. Jesus came to cast out those *demons* that imprisoned people.

Good News

What do people wish for? What do they want to do? Live life to the fullest? Be faithful to God? Find happiness? Sing for joy? Be set free from evil? Go forward in hope? Make others happy? Love and be loved? The Good News is this: Jesus shows the way to all these.

With Jesus

He came for people
in the dark of despair
to lead them to hope
in God's love and care.

He came for everyone
bowed down by pain.
He gave them courage
for life again.

He shared the struggle
everyone must face,
to make sure that evil
is given no place.

He asks, "Will you come
and work with me,
to fight the self-centeredness
evil wants to see.

"Will you build
in answer to my call,
a world of compassion
for one and all:
where all are free
and each walks tall?"

CHAPTER 2

A Leper

Byzantine mosaic from the end of the twelfth century. Jesus curing crippled and blind people.

Mosaics were the picture books of the church at a time when most people could not read. What would people learn from this picture?

© Giraudon - Cathedral of Monreale, Sicily (Italy)

Unclean! Unclean!

A carnival in Martinique

In Jesus' day a leper's life was desperate. Leprosy is a skin disease that eats away at the skin and cripples the body so badly that body parts may fall off. Some lepers looked disgusting and made people look away. People didn't know how to treat the disease. They were afraid of catching it. According to the Law of Moses, lepers had to live outside the towns and shout out "Unclean! Unclean!" to keep people away. People usually linked leprosy with sin and evil. Today medical science understands more about this disease. In Jesus' day the people with all sorts of skin diseases, like blotches and boils, were called lepers. So it was important, in every case, for someone to know whether they were dealing with a leper. If a person got better, someone had to declare that the illness was really cured. Today we would ask a doctor to do that. At the time of Jesus, the priests had to decide. During his lifetime in Judea, Jesus met many lepers. He did not reject them. He helped them to find their place again in society.

Cuban sculpture of a mother comforting her sick child

Matthew's Good News*

The way Jesus behaved toward lepers made an lasting impression on people. Memories of lepers being cured were told in the Gospels according to Mark, Luke and Matthew. Matthew collected ten stories of cures and put them in the same chapter. Even though it was forbidden to have any contact with a leper, Matthew says, "Jesus touched them."

In his accounts Matthew shows that these sick people spoke to Jesus in the same words that the first Christians used for their prayer: "Lord, have mercy!" or "If you want to, you can cure me."**

* Matthew
Matthew's Gospel was probably written between A.D. 80 and 90. He wanted to show that Jesus made time to talk with all people, including those who were sick and diseased.

** Other healings
After the healing of the leper (Matthew 8) we read about the healing of a centurion's servant, Peter's mother-in-law, some people in the crowd, two people troubled by "demons," a paralyzed man, a sick woman, an official's daughter, two blind people, and a man who was unable to speak.

If You Want To, You Can Make Me Clean!

Matthew 8.1-4

As Jesus came down the mountain, he was followed by large crowds. Suddenly a man with leprosy came and knelt in front of Jesus. He said, "Lord, you have the power to make me well, if only you wanted to."

Jesus put his hand on the man and said, "I want to! Now you are well." At once the man's leprosy disappeared. Jesus told him, "Don't tell anyone about this, but go and show the priest that you are well. Then take a gift to the temple just as Moses commanded, and everyone will know that you have been healed."

Mountain

Just as God's word was given to Moses on Mount Sinai, so Jesus spoke the words of good news on a mountain in Galilee. *"God blesses those people who grieve. They will find comfort!"* Jesus' healing was a sign that this was beginning to happen.

Don't Tell Anyone

The Gospels often tell us that Jesus asked people not to say anything about what he had done for them. He healed people to help them, not to get publicity.

Priests

Matthew is talking about priests who worked at the Temple in Jerusalem. They decided whether someone was cured of a disease or not, and they officiated at a ceremony in which the healed person was reincorporated into society.

Who Is Unclean?

Unclean

Sometimes people like to call other people "unclean." Often this means the poor, the homeless, prisoners, those who don't make the grade, or those who are different. People steer clear of them as if they were lepers and refuse to have anything to do with them. They turn their backs on such "unclean" people.

Invisible

We should think of such a thing as invisible leprosy. This disease shows itself in hateful and spiteful people. It sticks to the hands of those who won't share. It grows like scabs on the hearts of those who can't be bothered about God or their neighbor. It feeds off the wrong that people allow to go on around and in themselves. It doesn't scar the body but the heart!

Jesus Considers No One Unclean!

For Jesus, no one is unclean, not even a sinner! He touches and heals lepers to show publicly that God does not turn away from the "leprosy" which affects men and women. God loves everyone, in the same way: those who think they are clean as well as lepers!

Beauty Restored

When Jesus cures a leper, his or her face and body becomes beautiful again. The mission of Jesus was to do this for everyone. He helped people find ways to get rid of all the evil that spoiled their words and deeds and made their hearts ugly. Jesus makes it possible for each person to live as a beautiful child of God!

Make Me Clean!

People who have been infected with the "leprosy" of evil are not unclean forever. Jesus ignores no one. He will cure any kind of "leper" who comes along and says, "Without you, Lord, I'll be nothing but a leper. Help me ! Come and make me clean !"

Lepers All!

One way or another
we're all lepers!
No one is pure!
No one is better than everyone else!

Leprosy is on us and in us!
The leprosy of violence
gnaws at our hearts;
the leprosy of troublemaking
twists our mouths
taking away all beauty;
the leprosy of envy
burns like a fever in our eyes;
the leprosy of vanity
puffs up our words with pride!

How can we stop leprosy
from getting a stronger grip?
How can we stop it
from eating away inside us?

It's quite simple!
We only have to turn
toward Jesus the healer.
We only need to listen
to his urgent call and follow
the road of his Gospel of love,
love God and neighbor!

CHAPTER 3

A Blind Man

Nicholas Poussin
(1594-1665)
Curing the Blind
Oil on canvas

How do you know who are the most important figures in the painting?
Look at the expressions of the other people around them.
What do you think they are thinking and feeling?

© Photo R.M.N. - Louvre Museum, Paris (France)

Jericho

Present-day view of Jericho

Jericho* is a small town about twenty miles from Jerusalem. It is a comfortable oasis in a dry and treeless desert close to the Dead Sea. Herod had the town rebuilt to become a winter residence for the rich and famous of Jerusalem. There is plenty of water in Jericho, thanks to the springs and aqueducts. People call it "Palm Tree City." It's also a stopping place for pilgrims on their way to Jerusalem because it is only a day's journey away. At Jericho's city gate, you'll find beggars with arms outstretched to passers-by. These are the forgotten people of society. They have no money. Many are ill and have no one to help them. There's no such thing as Social Security. Among the beggars of Jericho is Bartimaeus, a blind man. Every day he sits there, hoping for a few coins. Today is going to be different!

Take Pity on Me!

Mark wrote this account of the healing of the blind** man for believers who had difficulty understanding fully who Jesus was. Like Bartimaeus, some people today need to be healed and saved. Like him, they understand easily enough that Jesus is the "Son of David." But there's more to it than that.

Like Bartimaeus, some people still have a lot to discover about Jesus, including why he was crucified and what it means to say "Jesus is risen."

Matthew and Luke also tell the story of this healing, but they do not name the blind man. Why does Mark call him "Bartimaeus" ("Son of Timaeus")? Perhaps it's because this man became a follower of Jesus and was known to many of Mark's readers.

* Jericho
Jericho is one of the oldest towns in the world. The site of the Israelites' miraculous victory over the Jebusites, as they entered the Land of Canaan, Jericho has been excavated by many archaeologists over the years. Nearby is the modern city of Jericho.

** Blind
In Jesus' day the Law of Moses said that blind people must be helped. But to be cured from blindness was a very rare thing and was considered a great miracle.

Remains of Herod's Palace in Jericho

15

Courage!

Mark 10.46-52

Jesus and his disciples went to Jericho. And as they were leaving, they were followed by a large crowd. A blind beggar by the name of Bartimaeus son of Timaeus was sitting beside the road. When he heard that it was Jesus from Nazareth, he shouted, "Jesus, Son of David, have pity on me!" Many people told the man to stop, but he shouted even louder, "Son of David, have pity on me!"

Jesus stopped and said, "Call him over!"

They called out to the blind man and said, "Don't be afraid! Come on! He is calling for you." The man threw off his coat as he jumped up and ran to Jesus.

Jesus asked, "What do you want me to do for you?"

The blind man answered, "Master, I want to see!"

Jesus told him, "You may go. Your eyes are healed because of your faith."

Right away the man could see, and he went down the road with Jesus.

Disciples

A disciple is someone who follows a particular teacher. Jesus chose twelve disciples: Peter, Andrew, James, John, and others. Since then everyone who tries to follow Jesus is thought of as a disciple.

Son of David

At the time of Jesus, many Jewish people were waiting for a liberator – someone to set them free. They called him the "Messiah" or "Son of David."

Rabboni or Teacher

This was an honorary name given to a teacher. The title "Rabbi" or "Rabboni" means "great master" or "my teacher."

Seeing Clearly

Loss of Sight

A blind person loses the sight of colors, trees, faces, the world, people, and things! Being blind is a terrible thing, but it's not a sign of sin or divine punishment. When Jesus cures the blind man at Jericho, he shows that no sickness is a punishment from God, and that God wants to free people from whatever their sickness or disease may be!

Being Blind

Even people with very good eyesight can sometimes be "blind." They can't see other people's problems, and they don't notice people smiling at them. They can't see what work needs to be done to make the world a better place. They see no further than themselves. They are blind!

Clear-sighted

We can all end up with this kind of inner blindness. The important thing is to be clear-sighted about it, not to think of ourselves as better than others, to watch out for the dangerous paths we sometimes walk along, and to be able to see the evil that sometimes wins out over us.

Help at Hand

How can we escape from the inner blindness that sometimes comes over us? How can we keep our hearts from closing? How can we see the road we need to take to be people who are fully open to God and others? It's difficult to do it all alone. Jesus Christ comes to our aid.

Counting on Jesus

Faith in Jesus overcomes inner blindness. He opens our eyes to see the direction the Gospel challenges us to follow. He opens our eyes so that we begin to notice our neighbors' hands stretched out in need. He gives us the courage to act in the way we know we should if we are being faithful to his word.

Recognizing Christians

How can you recognize
Christians ?
Who are the friends of Jesus ?

They believe in Jesus Christ,
and recognize in him
the Son of God
come down to earth.

They recognize in every man and woman
a brother and sister
belonging to the same human family,
loved by God, just like themselves.

They recognize that the love
they are called to show God and
their neighbor is one love.

They recognize that prayer
is not just words, but a way of living.

They believe that every day
Jesus Christ answers those who
trust in him;
and that evil can be overcome
by those who trust in Jesus
whole-heartedly.

They recognize that there is no
greater joy
than giving all of yourself
to making others happy.

CHAPTER • 4

A Tearful Widow

Resurrection of Lazarus
Attributed to Andronikos Byzagios
(Byzantine art from the middle
of the fifteenth century)

Can you recognize the main
characters of the story told
in this painting (Jesus, Lazarus,
Martha, Mary)? Look for the man
who is holding his nose.
What is he worried about?

20

© Ashmolean Museum, Oxford (England)

Nain

Present-day view of the village of Nain

The village of Nain was only a few miles from Nazareth where Jesus lived. Sadness filled this village as people came together for a funeral. The mother whose son was dead had now lost everything. Her husband was already dead, which made her a widow. She had no other children, which made her childless. She was completely alone and was vulnerable with no source of support. Her future seemed hopeless. The whole village came out to support her in her grief and to join the funeral procession.

Funeral procession in Guatemala

Some people present that day perhaps remembered the story in Scripture about the prophet Elijah written about 800 years before. When he was travelling in the same area, he had brought back to life the son of a woman who had given him a place to stay. People sometimes imagined dying was like going to sleep and only the Almighty God could wake them from the deep sleep of death.

Luke's* Good News

Luke is the only Gospel writer who tells the story of the widow of Nain. He probably wrote his Gospel between A.D. 70 and 80, about forty years after Jesus' ministry. As he went around preaching the Good News, Luke came across a lot of poverty and sadness. He understood more clearly what Jesus meant when he told us to welcome ordinary people, the poor, those who were unhappy, women, strangers, and social outcasts. In his Gospel, Luke wants to show how Jesus was always close to every person.**

In the story about raising the widow's son to life, nobody asked Jesus to do anything. It was Jesus who took the initiative. He didn't ask anyone to believe in him. He acted because he saw the weeping mother. By writing the story in this way, Luke invited his readers in the first century – and those of today – to be aware of and responsive to the suffering of others.

* Luke
Luke was a Gentile (a non-Jew) who became a Christian. He might first have been a doctor. He later traveled with Paul the apostle and learned all about the life of Jesus.

** Other cures
Luke reports some cures which are not found in the other Gospels: a sick man (14.1-6), ten lepers (17.11-19), the high-priest's servant (22.50,51), a woman who could not stand up straight (13.10-17).

B i b l e

Filled with Pity

Luke 7.11-16

Soon Jesus and his disciples were on their way to the town of Nain, and a big crowd was going along with them. As they came near the gate of the town, they saw people carrying out the body of a widow's only son. Many people from the town were walking along with her.

When the Lord saw the woman, he felt sorry for her and said, "Don't cry!"

Jesus went over and touched the stretcher on which the people were carrying the dead boy. They stopped and Jesus said, "Young man, get up!" The boy sat up and began to speak. Jesus then gave him back to his mother.

Everyone was frightened and praised God. They said, "A great prophet is here with us! God has come to his people."

News about Jesus spread all over Judea and everywhere else in that part of the country.

Filled with Pity

This phrase could mean "He had pity," or even better, "He was gripped by a strong feeling of deep sadness."

Get Up!

The way the man was raised to life again was different from the resurrection of Jesus. The young man was alive again, but eventually he would die once more. Jesus rises to a new life where there will be no more death.

Really Close

Grief

When someone we love dies, we feel the pain all the way to the bottom of our heart. It's as if the sun disappeared. Grief is one of the most terrible experiences we can ever have. In moments of grief, it seems that everything is collapsing, and that we will never be happy again. Each one of us will experience grief like this someday.

Many Kinds of Grief

Grief doesn't come only when a loved one dies. We experience grief when love grows cold, when we fail miserably, when sickness gets us down and ruins our plans for the future. We experience grief when a friendship or relationship dies. Whatever the cause, grief is always like a wound that does not heal.

Compassion

The word "compassion" means "suffering with" (com "with" plus passion "suffering"). It would be impossible to cope in times of grief if we did not have friends who were compassionate. They stay with us, they take some of the weight of our suffering, they comfort us, they help us hope again, and show that life will go on.

Filled with Pity

Jesus shows us how much compassion God has when we experience troubles and grief. God is close to those who are heartbroken, and is moved by the tears of those who have lost the reason for living. In the New Testament book of Revelation, we find the promise, "God will wipe every tear from their eyes."

Get Up

Throughout his life on earth, Jesus tried to take suffering out of people's lives, to lift them above whatever kept them sad, to wake them up from despair and bring them to that joy which God intends us all to have. He gave his life so that never again would we be overcome by the grief of death.

Let's Get Going!

It's not enough to be
moved by suffering.
It's easy to shed tears without
doing anything,
to bring comfort to those torn
apart by unhappiness.

Think about joining Jesus
to search out those who suffer
and are overcome by grief.
Let's go and tell them:
"We're here, close by
for you to lean on and get back your
strength."

Think about joining Jesus
to make time to listen to those life knocks
about
because they are poor,
because they have failed,
because they have sinned.
Let's go and tell them:
"We're here, close by for you
to lean on and get back your strength."

Think about joining Jesus
full of compassion,
to search out those who are
ready to give up
under the weight
of their troubles.
Let's go and tell them:
"We're here to help you
find joy again."

An Official's Son

St. John the Evangelist
Mosaic from the sixth century

The mosaic shows John with his special symbol, an eagle. Look for some other symbols in the picture. They will tell you about his great work.

© Giraudon - San Vitale Basilica, Ravenne (Italy)

In Galilee

Present-day view of the city of Nazareth

Here we are in the region of Galilee. It's a pleasant area with tree-covered mountains and a clear lake. Nazareth is in Galilee. Everyone knows that Jesus grew up there and spent his time there doing good, taking care of people's troubles and bringing them hope.

At Capernaum, a village on the lake, the son of a royal official is seriously ill. The official hears that Jesus, a fellow Galilean, has come home. Perhaps he could do something? The official leaves his home, taking the inland road from the lake for about eighteen miles, and meets up with Jesus at Cana. He is hoping that Jesus will come and cure his son. But Jesus does not plan to travel that day.

John's* Good News

John, who tells us this story, probably wrote his Gospel between A.D. 85 and 100, about fifty years after this event happened. Maybe he was there at Cana in Galilee. But then again, John doesn't intend to give a detailed account of what happened. He's not just writing a story; he's inviting his readers to believe** in Jesus. John does not talk about "miracles." He talks about "signs" that point people to a faith in Jesus. The cure of the official's son is the second sign that John reports. For him, what matters most is faith. The father believed that his son could be cured even at a distance, without Jesus going to visit him. After the healing, more people believed in Jesus.

Entrance to the village of Cana

Archaeological remains of the synagogue in Capernaum

* John
Some scholars think that John was one of the twelve disciples. Others disagree. John was clearly the youngest. He lived almost until the end of the first century A.D.

** Believe
Like us, John's readers sometimes found it hard to believe. He encourages them by telling them what Jesus said. "The people who have faith in me without seeing me are the ones who are really blessed!" (John 20.29)

Will You Ever Believe?

John 4.46-54

While Jesus was in Galilee, he returned to the village of Cana, where he had turned the water into wine. There was an official in Capernaum whose son was sick. And when the man heard that Jesus had come from Judea, he went and begged him to keep his son from dying.

Jesus told the official, "You won't have faith unless you see miracles and wonders!"

The man replied, "Lord, please come before my son dies!"

Jesus then said, "Your son will live. Go on home to him." The man believed Jesus and started back home.

Some of the official's servants met him along the road and told him, "Your son is better!" He asked them when the boy got better, and they answered, "The fever left him yesterday at one o'clock."

The boy's father realized that at one o'clock the day before, Jesus had told him, "Your son will live!" So the man and everyone in his family put their faith in Jesus.

This was the second miracle that Jesus worked after he left Judea and went to Galilee.

The Seventh Hour

At the time of Jesus, a day was divided into twelve hours from sunrise to sunset. The seventh hour corresponded to one o'clock in the afternoon.

Sign

Among the "signs" in John's Gospel are several healing stories: the man who had been ill for thirty-eight years (5.1-18), the man born blind (9.1-41) and the raising of Lazarus (11.1-44).

Believing

Proof

Some people say, "We'll believe in Jesus as long as we can have some proof that he's really God." It's as if they are forcing Jesus to defend himself and do what they want. It's a bit like bargaining. Believing in or loving someone has nothing to do with having proof. Believing in Jesus is trusting that he is God's Son as his earliest followers claimed.

Signs

Jesus does not offer proof, but he leaves signs. Jesus doesn't want to force anyone to believe! Here are some signs that help us believe in Jesus: Christians who love and forgive just as Jesus did, the Bible, and the memories and stories about Jesus.

Trust

Believing in Jesus means first of all trusting him or having confidence in him like the government official from Capernaum: "You've said you will. I trust your word. You will do it." Trusting Jesus means living according to the Good News, knowing that his message is the way to true happiness.

Prayer

Prayer depends on trust. We can talk to Jesus: "This is my life. These are my troubles. These are my joys. These are my difficulties. Come and help me. I give myself to you whole-heartedly." God always hears a prayer like this!

On the Road

Life's road is not always simple. There are good times and bad. There's loneliness and sadness. There's friendship and trouble. Jesus will always give signs to show he is present to those who trust him on life's road.

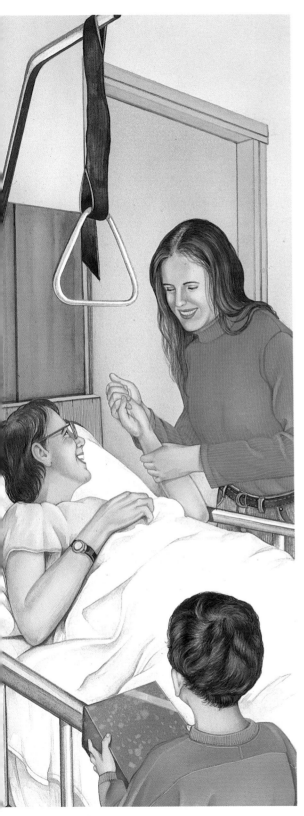

It's Jesus!

Do you recognize him?

At the touch of his hand
the leper's face is restored
to beauty;
those troubled by evil spirits
are restored to peace;
the paralyzed man can walk again.
The healing touch of Jesus
cured body and soul.
He brought good wherever he went.

Do you recognize him?

With his coming
people in the grip of sadness
are free to rejoice;
the dead to awake to new life;
people shattered by grief
find a shoulder to lean on.
The healing presence of Jesus
cured body and soul.
He brought good wherever he went.

Do you recognize him?

Jesus comforts the sick!
Mends broken hearts,
tenderly cares for everyone
crushed by suffering and sadness.
All who are doubled up
in despair
Jesus will set back on their feet.
He's the one!
Will you have faith
in him?

World Health

Many Diseases

There were about two hundred million people alive at the time of Jesus. Today we have reached six billion. There are also many more diseases. There are about thirty-one million blind people in the world (90% from poor countries). Some sickness gets better quickly like flu, colds, and indigestion, but other illnesses are more serious and can last a lifetime. This is the case with people who are disabled, paralyzed, blind, deaf, and unable to speak, and those who suffer daily with AIDS or cancer.

Where Does Sickness Come From?

We know today that sickness and disease do not come from some evil demon that has to be cast out. More and more we are discovering the cause of sickness and disease: viruses, bacteria, and even poor nutrition. But human beings are also responsible for causing and adding to the suffering of others in the world. Tobacco, drugs, alcohol abuse, road accidents, accidents at work, lack of hygiene, water and air pollution, senseless violence, and wars all bring misery into the lives of people. It's not enough to take care of sickness and diseases. We also have to try and root out what causes them.

Health Work

There are many fine hospitals in our country. You can find a doctor easily. Nurses are well trained. People are taken care of by Medicaid and Medicare. But it's not that way in all places of the world. In "developed" countries there are many more doctors and resources than in "underdeveloped" or poor, Third World countries.

A century ago, missionaries began to set up hospitals in some Third World countries: Albert Schweitzer in Gabon, Father Damien and Sr. Maryann in the leper colony of Molokai, and many others. Today there are organizations like The Red Cross that come to the aid of countries in need. The World Health Organisation (WHO) leads the battle against sickness and is active in sharing resources throughout the world.

Born in a Rich Country

Sally was born in a rich country. She was vaccinated. She eats when she is hungry. If she gets sick she is taken care of and is cured with proper medicine. She will be able to go to school, develop her mind and body, start a home and have her own children. If all goes well, she can hope to live until she is over eighty years old. Even then, she will be cared for.

Born in a Poor Country

Maria was born on the same day as Sally, but in a less developed country. She has a one-in-five chance of dying before her first birthday. She only has a one-in-five chance of being vaccinated and a one-in-four chance of ever learning to read and write. The water she drinks and the food she eats are often infected. If she gets sick, there is little chance of her being looked after by a health professional of any kind. If she has her own children, three or four of them will die before they reach the age of five. She can hope to live until she is maybe forty-five – that's thirty-five years fewer than Sally. Her country spends only a few pennies a year on her health. As the Third Millennium begins, there's still very much be done!

What Can I Do?

It's not good enough to sit and moan. We have to act. How ?
– visit those who are sick: talk to them, listen to them, make them happy;
– don't treat disabled people differently from others;
– think of a service career you could enter into in the future that would help reduce sickness or injustice;
– take part in action against hunger, against land-mines, against cancer;
– give assistance to people living in countries struck by epidemics or war.

Titles already published:

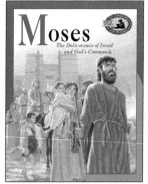

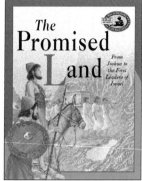

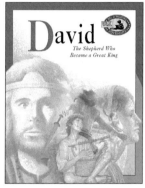

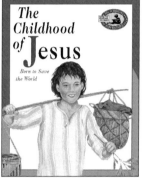

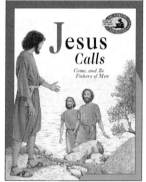

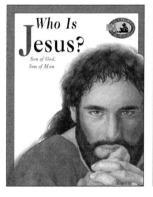

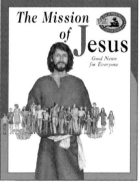

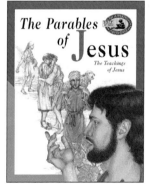

Forthcoming titles in the JUNIOR BIBLE Collection:

- The First Prophets
- Passion and Resurrection
- Exile and Return
- Isaiah, Micah, Jeremiah
- Jesus and the Outcasts
- Jesus in Jerusalem
- Acts
- Wisdom
- Psalms
- Women
- Revelation
- Letters

The Country of Jesus

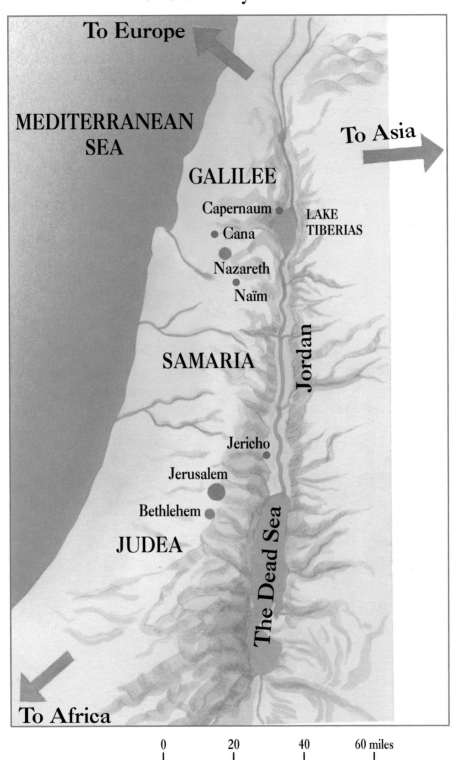

To Europe

MEDITERRANEAN SEA

To Asia

GALILEE

Capernaum

Cana

Nazareth

Naïm

LAKE TIBERIAS

SAMARIA

Jordan

Jericho

Jerusalem

Bethlehem

JUDEA

The Dead Sea

To Africa

0   20   40   60 miles

Jesus
Heals

ORIGINAL TEXT BY

Liam KELLY, Anne WHITE,

Albert HARI, Charles SINGER

ENGLISH TEXT ADAPTED BY

the American Bible Society

PHOTOGRAPHY

Frantisek ZVARDON

ILLUSTRATORS

Mariano VALSESIA, Betti FERRERO

MIA. Milan Illustrations Agency

LAYOUT

Bayle Graphic Studio

FIRST PRINTING: NOVEMBER 2000

Copyright © 2000 by Master Books
for the CBA U.S. edition.

For information write: Master Books, P.O. Box 727, Green Forest, AR 72638.

ISBN: 0-89051-330-9

ÉDITIONS
DU SIGNE
© ÉDITIONS DU SIGNE 1998